Dedicated to my everlasting friend, Ben
"It doesn't get any better than this!"

...and to those other benevolent barn swallows that make their nest at Green Trim Farm:

Beth, Aliza, Sarah, Laura, and Betsy

$2.00 from every sale of this book goes to the

Benjamin van Doren Hedges Memorial Scholarship Fund

a college scholarship fund for deserving students at

Souhegan High School in Amherst, New Hampshire

ISBN 0-9721489-1-4

UNIFIED BUSINESS TECHNOLOGIES PRESS
AMHERST, NEW HAMPSHIRE 03031

www.unifiedbiztech.com

Edited by Christina C. Schaller
and
B.J. Elliott

July 2002

10, 9, 8, 7, 6, 5, 4, 3, 2

Introduction

Not too long ago I calculated that a person working 40 hours a week averages a minimum of 35 percent of his waking weekly hours dealing with work. Just what is work? *Webster's New College Dictionary* defines work as: "Physical or mental effort or activity directed toward the production or accomplishment of something."

Webster's also defines work as "labor" among other things.

Given that we all "do work" in some fashion for a living and spend 35 percent of our week doing it, how many of us can honestly or accurately say we've achieved our work's purpose? Or to pose yet another question, how many of us can honestly or accurately say we know what the purpose of our work is—not just within the context of our daily activity, but within the bigger and broader context of a business itself? A good many of us might very well offer it would be really nice to know the answer to either of these questions. A few daring seekers of truth might be boldly honest enough to ask: How do I find out?

In order to find out, we have to go back to the definition of work. Not as *Webster's* defines it in just the sense of "labor" or "physical or mental effort," but as purposeful activity we *should be* doing to achieve a real and specific *purpose*—not just a "something."

Who wouldn't welcome the clarity of being able to both understand and see how the work they are doing has not only a defined purpose, but fits into the larger context of the business entity and its overarching purpose—its corporate reason for being?

Taking things to an even higher level—a spiritual level—how many of us are daily asking ourselves a similar question as it applies to our very reason for being—the purpose of our time here on Earth? For many of us the question is important and the answer is clear. But for equally as many others, the answer is as perplexing and mystical as the universe itself. An entire volume of books could be written in response to this question alone. This book isn't one of them.

Taking a Healthy Byte Out of the Tech-knowledgy Pie© is written for a less profound reason: to clarify the (often impractical) application and complexity of information technology in the workplace. To do this, however, we need to start with work—not just work in the sense we've already talked about it, but with *pure work*.

You won't find *pure work* defined in Webster's Dictionary—or probably anywhere else for that matter. *Pure work*, for the sake of business clarification, can be best described as the *effective* work of a company—work that carries a very real purpose and relates clearly to the *genesis* of the business. By *genesis* we mean the origins of the business and its reason(s) for coming into being. One might better explain *pure work* as the purposeful and real activities associated with things like making products, serving customers, and generating revenue—in short, the business lifecycle. An example of *pure work* stated simply in verb/object format with its specific purpose is:

- ◆ GET CUSTOMER (purpose): To identify a point of need in the marketplace that can be satisfied by a product we sell

Other examples of *pure work* activities are:

- ◆ OBTAIN PRODUCT
- ◆ DELIVER PRODUCT
- ◆ COLLECT PAYMENT

They are the *whats* and *whys* of the business that are central and core to its *effective* customer-centric performance, without the constraints of *how* the work gets executed (method and technology) or *who* executes the work (organization).

Long before the advent of the computer, people struggled with the complexities of business and the need to manage growth. Trying to see the "big picture" while maintaining a harmonious balance between a complex web of work processes, organization, and technology presented as much of a challenge to the Henry Fords and John D. Rockefellers of the early 1900s as it does to today's millennium-mavens of industry.

America's early business pioneers struggled with frustratingly limited, fragmented, and often myopic perspectives of their companies' work. As sales and production volume increased, so did infrastructure and bureaucracy. With growth, the *pure work* spawned by the original business purpose—the company's *genesis* if you will—became blurred or hopelessly lost in a quagmire of entangled, volume-driven complexity.

"So what's so different about that now?" Today's entrepreneurs amply aided (or some might say encumbered) by computer technology might ask.

One likes to believe we are better off with the introduction of the computer and the evolution of information technology. No one would dispute the marvels of Silicon Valley and the mega-leaps made in processing huge volumes of data at the speed of light. The data processing profession came into being as a result of mankind's need to automate. But are we better off if what we automate is the volume-spawned entanglement of forgotten purpose instead of a company's *pure work*—the *genesis* work that exists to fulfill the purpose of producing product and servicing customers?

Without a proper context, only chaos can prevail.

Regardless of the advent of information technology as a "science" or industry, today's business leaders and workers still face frustration in trying to understand the totality of their businesses—and more important—the *work* they *should be* doing to achieve the *purpose* of their businesses. Business purpose typically is manifested in the form of a stated (and preferably well thought out) strategic mission with accompanying goals and objectives.

Sometimes, however, the corporate purpose is forgotten, ignored, never clearly stated, or not stated at all. Neither is the *pure work* defined nor the operating data identified—the points of data origin and/or capture being either ignored or misplaced. Trying to build, buy, and implement information technology solutions without a clear contextual picture and understanding of *business purpose* or the *pure work*—the work employees *should be* doing to achieve the business purpose— can be likened to buying ingredients to bake a pie without first knowing what kind of pie to bake. Surprisingly, many people operate their businesses from an equally undefined position.

The majority of the commonsense business concepts appearing in this book were initially introduced to me by a man we'll call Samson Whitewater. Samson's influence on my own thinking about purpose and work (and their relationship to IT) has been significant. In his multi-decade quest to address the enigmas spawned by information technology, Samson—an IT professional himself—worked to bring the ever-evolving information technology industry, with its constantly changing cadre of technology solutions, into better alignment with the *real* needs of business.

The *purpose* of this book is to share and reinforce some commonsense concepts on how to do this without delving into the controversial depths of IT itself. As a long-tenured disciple of the concepts put forth in this volume I can attest to their efficacy. A more in-depth look at the concepts and controversies surrounding IT is planned as part of the upcoming adventure series of business clarification books to follow.

My own view of *purpose and work* has also been greatly influenced by another individual, but at a more spiritual level. That person is Ben Hedges—the man to whom this book is dedicated. Cut from cloth of a different weave and texture, Ben fulfilled his own purpose—his *life* purpose— within the realm of the human psyche. A clinical psychologist by profession, Ben dedicated his life to helping others find their way. Though not a "religious" man by nature or traditional definition, he put great emphasis on the spirit and the spiritual component of human nature. Financially independent, he chose to invest the better part of his life helping adolescent students. He fulfilled this purpose in his latter years through the role of a high school guidance counselor.

Perhaps further fueling his purpose in helping others find their own was the fifteen year battle he fought with Hodgkins Lymphoma. Although he eventually succumbed, physically, to the disease at the age of 51, his spirit never knuckled under to its debilitating effects. If anything, Ben's indomitable spirit grew deeper and stronger as a result of the fight. In a unique fashion, the burden that he carried gave him a stronger sense of purpose and infused the understanding he gave to others with greater potency and value. His life and the lives of those closest to him—his wife and four daughters—inspired the *human* context for *The Adventure of BarnSwallow Pies* that follows in a few pages.

The simple but powerful approach to rediscovering the essence or genesis of a business, illustrated through *The Adventure of BarnSwallow Pies,* originally evolved as a means to identify and capture *real* business requirements—the pure, purpose-driven work of a business—in preparation for designing and building customized information technology solutions. As such, the resulting business models and work-process flows (once considered byproducts) created through this methodology were typically set aside or discarded after the highly sought after points of data origin and capture had been dutifully identified.

It was through further discovery and evolution that other practitioners utilizing concepts from Samson Whitewater's approach eventually began leveraging the purpose-driven, *pure work* models as commonsense blueprints for total or holistic business design. To that end, read on and begin a journey that helps you discover the potential for realizing a state of *holistic business wellness* while perhaps reevaluating your own sense of purpose in the process.

Purpose and Work Provide the Context for the Entire Business

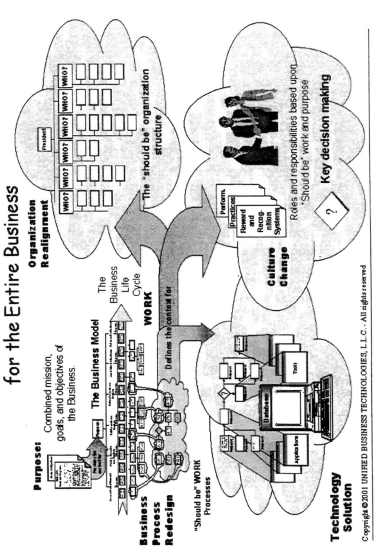

Purpose: Combined mission, goals, and objectives of the Business.

The Business Model

The Business Life Cycle

WORK

Defines the context for

Organization Realignment

President

WHO? WHO? WHO? WHO? WHO?

The "should be" organization structure

Business Process Redesign

"Should be" WORK Processes

Culture Change

Perform. Practices

Reward and Recognition Systems

Roles and responsibilities based upon "Should be" work and purpose

Key decision making

?

Technology Solution

Tools

Database

Application

The ADVENTURE of
BARNSWALLOW PIES

Priscilla BarnSwallow and husband, Bert, lived a happy life at BarnSwallow Farm with their daughters Bliss, Blush, Blythe, and Blanche. Life was simple and good.

"It doesn't get any better than this," Bert BarnSwallow would be known to proclaim on tranquil evenings when sunset draped BarnSwallow Farm in a mantel of paint-splashed color.

"Each of us has our own unique purpose to achieve," Bert would always say.

"...and each of us has *WORK* we *SHOULD BE* doing to achieve that purpose."

"Purpose drives work and work fulfills purpose."

And so it was that Bert spent many a worthwhile day fulfilling his purpose by doing the work that brought prosperity and success to Barn-Swallow Farm.

But as time moved on at the farm, Bert became ill and found it difficult to fulfill his purpose. He became confined to bed and grew weaker by the day.

Eventually Bert passed on. It was a
sad occasion at BarnSwallow Farm.

Finding herself widowed and on her own with four girls to raise, Priscilla began to feel overwelmed.

"How will we ever manage?" She wondered.

"All I know how to do is cook and raise a family. I can't run a farm."

"You make great pies, Mom!" Blythe BarnSwallow, the youngest of the girls, offered reassuringly.

"We could bake pies and sell them to earn money."

And so it began that Priscilla BarnSwallow began making pies.

The *PURPOSE* of Priscilla's business was:

TO BAKE ARTFULLY FLAVORFUL PIES OF SUPERIOR QUALITY TO SELL AT A PROFIT.

She worked diligently day and night.

"This is getting ridiculous," Priscilla complained to her girls.

"It takes me two hours to complete one pie. I'm only turning out seven pies a day. At $7.00 a piece that's not very much money."

"We could all help, Mom," Blanche BarnSwallow suggested.

"With four of us plus you baking pies, we could probably bake at least 35 pies a day. That's a pretty significant increase in production," daughter Blush offered.

BARN SWALLOW PIES, INC.

And so the growth of BarnSwallow Pies began. As the pies sold, demand for the artfully baked and flavorful pies grew. Soon more production had to be added. To accommodate the increase, Priscilla BarnSwallow converted the old barn into a factory. She hired a dozen local townspeople to work the factory and cranked up production to 1500 pies a day. Business was good and the money came pouring in.

In order to support the growing business, Priscilla contracted with a large computer firm to manage the computer technology.

The name of the company was:

Big Business Underwriters Korporate Computer Systems—BIG BUCKS for short.

BIG BUCKS loaded up BarnSwallow Pies with every new technology offering they developed.

"You've got to adapt your business to fit the technology," *Big Bucks* salesman Dasdee P. DisqueDrive said.

"It's the only way you can stay ahead of the competition. Just about everybody else is doing it. It's the latest thing! You have to do it if you want to grow," Dasdee insisted.

So BarnSwallow Pies grew to be an enormous corporation. The once simple barn expanded to incorporate a huge factory. Priscilla BarnSwallow found the demands of handling the growth overwhelming. She hired specialists to run the various departments that had sprung up. She had an operations VP, a human resources VP, a marketing VP, an accounting VP, and *two* VPs of information technology.

As the business continued to grow, operating costs did too—in fact they grew at a rate that far exceeded sales.

Priscilla's expert VPs defended the budgets for their departments un-waveringly. As sales of BarnSwallow Pies continued at a healthy rate, profit fell dramatically.

"We need to automate our work processes with new technology," the two VPs of IT insisted.

"Business today has become too complex. And IT is extremely sophisticated. Why don't you put *us* in charge of running the business?" VP Spooler suggested.

"IT is the way of the future. It's the only way to fix the problem," VP DataDump added.

Priscilla BarnSwallow was *not* happy!

That night Priscilla shared her business dilemma with her four daughters around the kitchen table.

"Everything is out of control ...and everything has gotten so complicated! Life was much simpler when just the five of us baked pies. It seems like the larger the volume got, the more complex the business became. Now I can't make sense of *any* of it!" Priscilla lamented.

"Well, I'd go back to what Dad used to say about *purpose* and *work*," daughter Bliss recollected.

"Purpose drives work and work fulfills purpose."

"Why don't you start there by revisiting the *purpose* of BarnSwallow Pies? Then figure out the *work* you *should be* doing to achieve that purpose."

That night when Priscilla went to bed, her late husband, Bert, appeared in a dream and described the things Priscilla needed to do to restore order to BarnSwallow Pies.

Bliss was right! Everything began with *purpose*.

"You have to rediscover the *genesis* of your business," Bert told Priscilla in her dream.

BARNSWALLOW PIES
OUR BUSINESS PURPOSE: TO BAKE Artfully Flavorful PIES of superior Quality to SELL AT A PROFIT!

To that end, Priscilla organized and ran special facilitated work sessions that communicated the business purpose of BarnSwallow Pies to everyone.

But she wondered how she would unravel the complicated web of organization, work-processes, and information technology that had evolved over the years at the company.

The company culture had changed too—for the worse.

"Start with the *what* and the *why*," Bert told Priscilla in another of what would become a series of informative dreams.

"Get a small, knowledgeable group of workers and managers together, then build a *work-model* of the business."

"Forget about the *who* and the *how* to start–that can come later ...and identify the *data* you need to make and sell pies too," Bert added.

BARNSWALLOW PIES
GLOSSARY OF BUSINESS TERMS
• CUSTOMER –
• PRODUCT –
• AVAILABILITY –
• ON ORDER –
• ON HAND – "SHOULD BE"
WORK MODEL:
PURPOSE
That's Not How I DEFINE "Customer", milton
IDIOT

During the modeling sessions, things were sometimes intense. A *glossary of business terms* needed to be built out to ensure a common understanding of the work.

People like Milton MissileLauncher grew angry and impatient over the process. But Priscilla stayed calm and worked through problems with dignity and poise.

BARNSWALLOW PIES
WHAT and WHY ONLY
BUSINESS PURPOSE
"SHOULD BE" WORK MODEL
DATA!
DATA!

Thus with no small amount of effort, Priscilla facilitated a diverse group of her best business people through the construction of a verb/object *work-model*—the work that BarnSwallow Pies *should be* doing to achieve its business purpose. The *work-model* was constructed without worrying about *who* should do the work or *how* it would get done.

They identified the *data* needed to support the work too.

Priscilla and her group of business specialists organized the *work-model* they'd built into *logical process work-flows*.

Since the *work-model* contained only the *pure work* needed to make and sell pies—in other words the support and administrative work had been stripped out—a series of *should be* process-flows detailing the *how* was relatively straightforward to build.

The *data* needed was mapped to the work-flows too.

58

For the first time since the company began, Priscilla BarnSwallow had a precise roadmap of the *work* Barn-Swallow Pies *should be* doing to achieve its business purpose—down to the actual data capture transaction level.

She also knew the exact data she needed to run her pie business. Using these very specific business requirements, she tasked IT VPs DataDump and Spooler to summon *Big Bucks* salesman, Dasdee P. DisqueDrive to formulate an IT solution.

As a result, Spooler and DataDump proposed an application suite combination of homegrown and packaged IT solutions to run BarnSwallow Pies. The business people were intimately involved in the decision and selection processes too.

Since everyone now knew the exact requirements of the business, a streamlined and accurate IT solution was implemented. This resulted in a significant reduction in both hardware and systems support.

Needless to say, Dasdee P. Disque-Drive was *not* particularly happy!

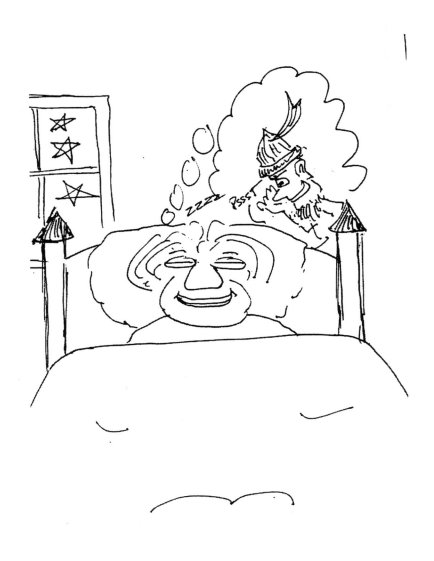

Once again Bert came to Priscilla in a dream and spoke to her.

"Don't forget to put the *who* back into the equation," Bert whispered softly.

"...and *reward* people on how well they achieve the *purpose* of the work they *should be* doing."

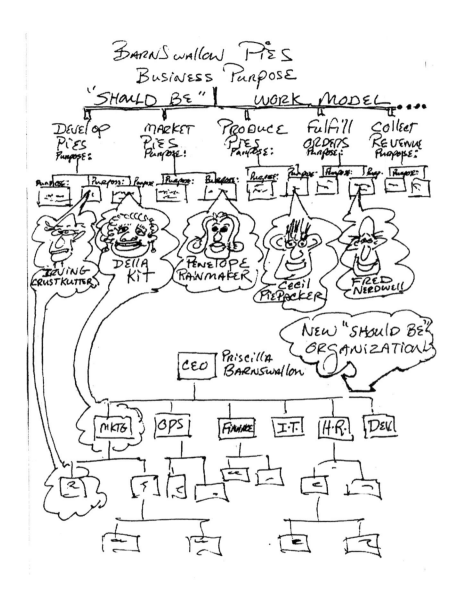

64

Following Bert's advice, Priscilla and her team of business modelers mapped the entire organization of BarnSwallow Pies to the *work* and *work-process models* they'd created. From there it was easy to make decisions about the *who* part of the business.

The entire organization was realigned to reflect and support the *should be work* of BarnSwallow Pies.

Additionally, since each specific work activity now had a very exacting purpose associated with it, Priscilla and her modeling team defined performance measurements representative of achieving the various work purposes.

The human resources team then implemented a new reward system that more accurately rewarded workers for their contributions.

Everybody was a *lot* happier—that is except for information technology VP Spooler whose job could now be eliminated.

Purpose and Work Provide the Context for the Entire Business

And so it was that Priscilla Barn-Swallow (with her late husband, Bert's, help) redesigned and restructured BarnSwallow Pies into an orderly manifestation of its business purpose—its *genesis*.

It wasn't long thereafter that BarnSwallow Pies began turning a tidy profit.

The employees and customers were all a lot happier too as customer service and morale surged to new heights.

70

But that wasn't the end of Priscilla's nocturnal visits with her late husband.

Because of Bert's relentless integrity and insightful grasp of the spiritual, the lessons Priscilla learned about *purpose* didn't stop with business.

effectively applied unless it too incorporates and supports the *purpose* and *pure work* of the business enterprise. *The Adventure of Barn-Swallow Pies* provides a simple illustration of the importance of purpose and work in setting the critical context for IT solutions. Ultimately, until we penetrate the cloud of technology often applied to symptoms—and sometimes masking the root cause misalignment of purpose and work—we will never successfully design, build, purchase or implement effective information technology solutions.

What other cloud dispersing adventures lie ahead? The business world is ripe with mystical fruit in need of thought-provoking clarification before its benefits can be properly harvested. A few of the challenging topics slated for enlightenment during the course of this millennium are:

- Clarifying International Business
- Clarifying Leadership
- Clarifying the Computer
- Clarifying the Organization
- Clarifying the Internet
- Clarifying Corporate Culture